The Indie Author's
NO BULLSHIT GUIDE
To Marketing on a BUDGET

Written by twelve time (Independently) published fiction author, Ava Abernathy, oops! I mean, Dianah Brock

© 2021 Ava Sprayberry Abernathy, publishing under the pseudonym Dianah Brock.

All Rights Reserved.

No portion of this book may be printed, reproduced, quoted without the expressed written consent of the author, except for short quotes with citation for essays, journals, articles. To request using more than one passage of quote for reference, please email your request to Dianah_Abernathy@outlook.com or by using the contact us box at www.Abernathybooks.com

Disclaimer

This book happened completely by accident! One day, I sat down at my desk to write out my marketing strategy for the upcoming weeks. Before I knew it, one section led to another, then another, and finally another. Before I knew it, I had sat down and filled a composition book over half full of hand written procedures.

That being said, I cannot prove the process detailed in this book. I can tell you that the procedures, processes, ideas, and tactics shared within these pages are direct results of approximately 15 months of rigorous, aggravating, and beyond stressful marketing attempts. This book is a product of trial and error. Each process, tip, and technique has shown results for me.

Allow me to reiterate, I **CANNOT** prove that this well organized, thought out process, presented in this order will work for you. In fact, this book launch will be a test run for the process.

Prior to sitting down and constructing this title, this "process" was nothing more than disorganized chaos within the mental filing cabinet in my brain that I finally sat down and organized. So, I cannot promise it will work for you, but I can promise you, this is really a no bullshit guide, compiled of not only my own successes, but my own failures as well.

In closing, I am not liable for any losses you may have. You are gambling here with this process, just as I am. However, life is a gamble, and I am glad that I rolled the dice, and I hope that you will be too. As you read through the information in this book, you will find that the key ingredient to anything I share with you will be commitment to your work. This book also contains adult language. Just thought I would throw that out there ☺

PLEASE READ THIS BOOK ENTIRELY BEFORE PLANNING ANYTHING!!

Goals

Before you dive down deep into the knowledge that this book has to offer, I would recommend making some notes, answering a few questions, and laying your expectations for the information in this book. That is why I have provided some study prep for you on this page.

GOALS:

_____
_____
_____
_____
_____
_____
_____
_____
_____
_____
_____
_____
_____
_____
_____
_____
_____

Introduction

I published my first novel, *The Story of Michelle Brown Vandivere* in 2010 with a vanity press publishing company called *Publish America LLC*. I was twenty-five years old at the time, and I had stars in my eyes as I signed that seven year contract. I won't lie, I thought that zero dollar advance contract, with 12% royalty and 20% discount for author's stock would have me drinking tea with Stephen King within a year.

Boy, oh boy, was I wrong!

So what did that contract offer me? That contract gave me seven years of a publishing company sending weekly emails, trying to pimp my own books out to me. Here is the problem with that, and quite frankly, what pissed me off about the situation. I wasn't making any money. They didn't assist me with marketing or promoting in any way. I didn't have a publicist scheduling appearances and book signings for me. So they tried to make money by selling me copies of my own book.

Did I try to market my book myself? That depends on who you are asking. If you ask 25 year old star struck me, she would tell you "Oh yes! I post on My Space and Facebook at least ten times a day!" If you ask me now, the version of me that has researched the market, how publishing works, etc. I would tell you, "Hell no! That idiot thought that she would post about a book release once and all of her family and friends would spend their last 24.99 for a 220 page paperback just to show support. What a dumb ass."

Within six months of my release, I realized that book wasn't going anywhere. So what did I do? I told myself it would be better with my next book since I would be independently publishing and I would have total control. I would contact the retail stores and make the deals to put the trial run on the shelves. I would contact the radio stations and news stations local to me, because a published author, independent or not from a small down with a population of 646 people was one hell of an accomplishment, right? They didn't think so. So what did I do over the course of the next nine years, and 12 titles?

↓*THIS IS NOT A PLAN FOR SUCCESS*

1. I published a book.
2. I made a few posts on social media.
3. Then, did NOTHING!

↑*THIS IS NOT A PLAN FOR SUCCESS*

When my health took a turn for the worse in early 2019, my husband and I knew that I would no longer be able to hold down a regular job. Office positions are not really a thing where we live, and that left my only option as anything that required me to stand and walk for 6 to 12 hours a day, five to six days a week. I had worked in direct sales since I was nineteen, and used those network marketing companies to supplement my income, but it never really made me one of the company elite sellers that appear on their recruiting videos.

One night, my husband and I were sitting on the front porch of our rented single wide trailer talking about my plan to invest getting back into direct sales and network marketing. I had also mentioned that I wished my books would do something but they just sat there in Amazon world. That is when my husband asked me the question that lit a fire under my ass.

"Why would you want to invest money to sell products to give the majority of what you make to a multi-million dollar company when you could invest it in your own products?"

LIGHT FUCKING BULB!

As anyone who has ever worked in direct sales and network marketing knows, while you can invest a lot of money into trying to make it work, you will invest far more **TIME** than anything else. My husband had a point. If I was going to invest money, and my precious time into trying to sell a product, why didn't I try to sell a product that I created? One that I believed in? It made perfect sense! In April of 2019, Abernathy Books was born. I began marketing my work, got started with audio books, and built a brand that I could be proud of, and keep building.

    This book is going to cover very important aspects of the independent publishing world. While the creative freedom authors have in this method is fantastic, it also requires a lot of work if you have bigger plans than simply filling an Amazon Kindle Direct Publishing bookshelf. If you want to see a return, and have that email come in with a royalty payment statement, then you have some work to do.

So sit back, grab a cup of coffee, some form of alcohol to spike it with, and possibly some anti-anxiety medication, because you are going to need all of it as I tell you what you need to know, and then share a book launch process with you. First item on the agenda? I am going to tell you the truth about marketing. Understanding these truths will prepare you to successfully launch your book, which is the ultimate goal of this book.

Part One

The Truth about Marketing

Let's dive right in. There are three primary truths about marketing.

1. **It's time consuming**
2. **It isn't free.**
3. **It requires a platform**

Yes, I am sure you have seen the ads all over social media with authors and content creators trying to sell you their course about how to "effectively market your book in as little as one hour," or "in the time it takes you to drink your morning coffee." I have seen these ads full of false promises and when I see them, I am tempted ask these content creators "Which hour are we talking about?" or "How many cups of coffee do you consider to be 'morning' coffee?"

The truth is, while you can find legitimate courses, resource materials, books, etc. all over the internet that will help you gain the knowledge you need, most of these paid ads you see on Facebook that promise to take the work out of book marketing is nothing more than someone blowing smoke up your ass. It's a way to make a quick buck or two, and they really don't care if you become successful or not.

 Have you seen an ad recently promoting the "100% free marketing guide" that will "guarantee you results?" Yeah, me too, and guess what? That isn't free either. You pay for the guide, even if it is only a shipping and handling fee, and odds are, you will find that some of the resources they share with you are paid resources. Marketing isn't free, and as we go in depth on this just ahead, you will learn why even if you spend nothing monetarily for the resource, it still isn't free.

 Here is one of my personal favorites; "Buy my course now, and I will tell you everything you need to know about getting booked for events to build your platform!" Yes, I agree, you absolutely, 100% need an author platform to generate any level of success at all. However, a course that you pay 50.00 for, and it turns out to be nothing more than a series of You Tube videos is not only deceptive, but it is also a waste of your money.

Now that I have told you the three primary truths about marketing, let's get down and dirty while I break it down for you and explain the sub-truths associated with each one.

Truth One: It's Time Consuming

So, here are the facts; Marketing is time consuming because effective book marketing:

- ➤ **Requires consistency**
- ➤ **Requires planning**
- ➤ **Requires record keeping**
- ➤ **Requires research**

I know at this point, you are probably asking yourself, "What the hell did I get myself into?" Well, let me tell you. You have a book, and you have a dream to see that book out in the world. In order to do that, without the hassle querying literary agents, and big name publishing houses, you have to put in the work.

In order to put in the work, you need to be consistent with your efforts, you need to plan according to your schedule so that you do not overlap your responsibilities, you need to keep a record of what you have done, what you have spent, contacts you have made, and lastly, finding all of the information you need to effectively market your book and have it ready for launch, requires hours of research.

Consistency

What do you need to be consistent with? The answer is absolutely everything! However, to give you an example of consistency, allow me to paint a picture for you. My author platform consists of a website with a blog, an online store, You Tube channel, Facebook author page, a Facebook group for readers, (Abernathy Books Reader's Community) Instagram, and Twitter. These sites all build my author platform. I am able to reach out to readers who enjoy watching videos on You Tube, I have a blog for those readers that want to know more about me.

Consistency comes into play with each of these platforms that build Abernathy Books as a whole. For instance, if I post on my Facebook page that I have released a new audio book, then my followers on Facebook know to go to You Tube or my website to watch the book trailer. I post to my author page at least every other day, although for some of you that may get your hands on this book later, I am guaranteed to have reached my daily posts goal.

You may be wondering why it is so important to post to social media accounts daily, or to post to your blog weekly. Well, the answer is simple. You don't want your audience to forget about you. You want them to know that yes, you are still actively writing, you have a new book coming out, you have a contest going in your fan group, so on and so forth. The less present you are online, the less you and/or your book are on the minds of readers and potential readers. The more involved you are, the more your following will grow, and the more people will engage with you. Now, I could go on and on about consistency, but I don't want to bore you. You will get and in depth look at consistency with the book launch plan ahead.

Planning

Honestly, anyone with clear goals in mind knows that planning is a requirement for succeeding in their goals. The same goes for marketing your book. You need to know an approximate date that you book will launch, schedule that launch, make time to work on knew projects, have time to write that new blog post, or make that book trailer. Literally everything in life requires planning, and that goes double for marketing.

The planning phase works hand in hand with consistency. An example of my planning is, I like to schedule my page posts on social media up to seven days in advance. This time devoted to planning out my posts actually frees up a lot of my time for writing new books, outlines, or even planning my next launch. I mean, let's face it, a lot of indie authors are also working regular jobs, and the last thing you need to do is be stressing over social media announcements, or contest deadlines while you are on the clock at your regular nine to five.

I love calendars. I use my calendar on my laptop, I have a planner that I write in, and I even have a weekly planner that I write down what book gets promoted on what day of the week. Since I keep track of what I have going on, and what I have coming out, I am able to plan my activities accordingly on a daily basis to achieve the best results possible. I mean, let's face it; organized chaos is better than disorganized chaos.

I am also a big fan of lists. I have a habit of ending each day with making a list of what I need to do the next day, and placing that list on my computer keyboard. We will give better examples of planning in the book launch section later on, but right now, this is the short version.

Note Now would be a good time to get your hands on a planner, and start getting in the routine of planning. You have a lot of work to do.

Record keeping

Are you feeling as though you are running a home-based internet business yet? If so, then great. That means that we are getting somewhere with this information, and you know that if you are going to have a successful book launch, you are going to need to put in the work.

So what records do you need to keep? The short answer is everything, but if the short answer was good enough, we wouldn't need a book to help guide us through launch process, and marketing now, would we? I know that you may not publish in every format that I do, or do things the exact way that I do, but for example's sake, we will use my book biz as a reference.

Aside from my author website for blogging and information, I also operate an online store that sells official book and author merchandise related to my titles. Part of my record keeping is keeping track of money spent on stock, shipping fees, sales tax, etc. I also keep a record of how much of what I have in stock, and when I run a free Kindle book promotion, I keep a daily written record at my desk for quick access.

I am also deep into audio books. If audio books are new for you, then allow me to share some info. If an author uses ACX to produce audio books, and those books are produced with a royalty share option, then ACX will provide promo codes to the author and narrator to distribute to reviewers. I keep a record of who receives codes, whether or not they have reviewed. Basically, the: who, what, where, why, when, and how of sharing those codes. I do this as it allows me to follow up and get those reviews that are vital to building my following.

I also keep a record of money spent on paid ads, the stats for those ads, and what type of ad I ran. For example, if I decided to run a five day paid ad on Facebook using an edited promo photo, then I will track how effective that ad was compared to an ad with say, a book trailer. Doing this will allow me to see what is working for me, and what my readers are responding to.

In summary, record keeping is primarily about money spent, and money earned. We will go into greater detail about what you may want to have on hand prior to a book launch in order to track your efforts. As I have said, my marketing process is a result of trial and error. It is easier for me to utilize the data from that trial and error process if I have a nice, organized, and informative reference to look at while I am in the planning stage of my next promotion.

Research

Ah, that wonderful step in book plotting, planning, and writing that every author is all too familiar with. Well, it is also a key process in creating a marketing plan for your new release. Research is literally ground into every aspect of this business, and unfortunately, it doesn't stop when pen meets paper on your manuscript. If you are an independent author, (as I am sure you are considering you are reading this book now) research is even more crucial.

So, what do you need to research? The first answer to this question would be, "I need to research how to effectively market my work." The first answer is of course, the obvious one. Lucky for you, I am answering that question for you, or rather, I will remind you of the key component to writing.

In school, when our teachers were teaching us about the writing process, they taught us how to plot. Plotting consisted of gathering the very basic information for those five paragraph, five sentence minimum essays that were due on Friday. This process consisted of answering six very important questions:

1) Who?
2) What?
3) Where?
4) Why?
5) When?
6) How?

These six, one word questions are always the beginning, but without a topic, they are impossible to answer, that is where the teacher came in; providing a topic that you were to write about, and we would do the rest. For role playing (as well as education's sake) I will take on the role of teacher, and you, the reader, will be my student. Therefore, allow me to make these questions a little easier to answer. Remember, we are researching marketing for your book, so that is your topic.

1. Who is my target audience?
2. What genres are popular right now?
3. Where can I find my target audience?
4. Why is this location the best place to market my book?
5. When will be the best time to launch in order to reach my goals?
6. How will I grab their attention and persuade them to buy my book?

As you can see, the plotting stages are the same, but the questions that you need to answer are more detailed and will give you, the author a bit more knowledge to plan a book launch, and (fingers crossed) successful marketing strategy. Another detail you may have noticed is that the questions focused more on your projected or target audience more than they focused on your book. There is a legitimate reason for that, and the reason is quite obvious:

HARD TRUTH: IT ISN'T ABOUT YOUR BOOK ANYMORE! THE FOCUS IS ON YOUR AUDIENCE NOW!

Don't worry, your book will regain the spotlight later on. I mean, we are discussing making your book a huge focal point for an entire five day launch right?

Now that I have shared with you, the right questions to ask, I am going to teach you the right way to answer these questions. Much like that essay assignment in school, your marketing research, or plotting has a clear goal, and that goal is book sales. However, before we go that far, we need an example. Therefore, we will be using one of my own books to answer the questions mentioned above.

PROJECT: The Apocalypse Diaries: The Fall

1. **What is my target audience?** Zombie fans. Probably age range 18-40 years old. Anyone who loves the supernatural, suspense thrillers, or books about a world apocalypse.
2. **What genres are popular right now?** Romance, erotica, suspense, and sci-fi.

TIP: To answer this question, scroll through a few Facebook groups, or look at the current best-seller list on Amazon. Maybe even pay attention to those annoying book ads about shapeshifter romance.

How do the current popular genres compare to your book?

COMPARE

I know, I know, it sounds crazy. You're probably thinking, "How in the hell is she going to compare a zombie apocalypse book to a shapeshifter romance novel?" My author brain could tell you, but then I may lose some readers, and quite frankly, that type of shifting romance wouldn't settle well with my stomach, and probably not yours either. So, allow me to show you how I think outside the box when figuring out how I can get my book on as many platforms as possible, and

Shapeshifter Romance	Zombie Apocalypse
Supernatural	Supernatural
Romance	Romance? (Is it there?)
Suspense	Suspense
Violence	Violence
Sexual content	Sexual content
Tragedy	Tragedy
Emotions	Emotions

into as many genres as possible. After all, I am considered a multi-genre author. ☺

POP QUIZ? What is this process called? You guessed it! It is the Compare and Contrast method. Now that we have compared the similarities, let's contrast them.

Having Ideas? Jot them down:
_____
_____
_____
_____
_____
_____

CONTRAST

Shapeshifters	Zombies
Shifter/Shifter or Shifter/Human relationship	Relationships will usually be two humans
Will the pack alpha choose the meek human?	Will the romantic relationship survive the ordeal?
Sexual content is primarily always in these books.	It can be done. Did you do it? I did.
Were-woman is usually forced into a relationship when she is in love with someone else.	People closest to the main character have a higher chance of dying.
Emotions are usually always love, loneliness, and longing, or heartbreak.	Fear, love, need to survive just to name a few.

*** Before we move on to question three, I feel it is necessary to note here that after the compare and contrast exercise, the author should find that their book fits into a multitude of genres, at least three. So, jot those down for future reference when assigning your keywords and genres on your publishing platform.

3. **Where can I find my target audience?**

   - Once you have done the compare and contrast exercise, a lot of those words are

keywords. Start searching Facebook, and join a lot of groups. Join everything you can get into, but read the rules first. Some groups have rules about no self-promotion. Also join all of the garage sale/yard sale sites you can find. Those will come in handy later.
- Next, you will want to follow author pages. No, you won't be able to advertise your books on their pages, but if your ad is catchy enough, they may share your posts for you.
- Now, hit the internet and find every single blogger, vlogger, and podcaster you can find. Odds are, they need you as much as you need them.

4. **Why are these locations the best place to advertise my book?** I will tell you why. It's what they do. They are trying to grow

their platforms to monetize them, and they need people just like you to help them do that. Utilize their platforms and they will not disappoint you.

5. **When is the best time to launch my book?**
   The truth is, you can launch a book at any time, but the time of year you choose to do so could have an impact on sales results. For example, If I were to release The Apocalypse Diaries: The Fall in the summer (I did, and it was a struggle.) it may not generate the sales it could have generated had I released it in Spooky Season, AKA October. So the timing is crucial. If your genre is romance, consider a launch in late January so that it can be given as a gift when Valentine's Day rolls around.

6. **How will I grab the attention of my target audience and persuade them to buy my**

book? Well, there are a few things that you can do here. One, is book trailers. There are independent artists out there looking to make money, and they offer discounted book trailers at a reasonable price. Also, explore your laptop. You may have video editing software standard on your PC. As for video clips, I like to use www.Pixabay.com. Their content is free to use, but they do incorporate a donate button. Use it as often as you can and compensate the artist for their work. You don't write books to give away for free, and they shouldn't be expected to provide cover art, video clips, or audio for free either. So in short:

- Book Cover photo with a review
- Book Trailer, reading the synopsis
- A low volume copyright free music or audio as background.

To recap, since this is a very long section with a ton of information:

- Make a list of local media (newspapers, radio stations, book stores, libraries, and any other location with a public bulletin board for flyers.
- Remember, there are a lot of bloggers, vloggers, podcasters, and social media influencers looking for content. So add those to your list of media outlets to contact when launch time rolls around.

Finally, and I saved this for last, you need to research paid ads, specifically with Facebook, Twitter, Instagram, and Amazon. This closing leads directly into the next truth, but first, let's takes some notes!

As briefly as possible, explain everything that you have learned about the first truth.

_____
_____
_____
_____
_____
_____
_____
_____

Remember the six important questions to ask when writing or planning anything.

- **Remember that compare and contrast is more than essay writing in school assignments. It can literally be the tool that defines whether or not your new book, or business will/can succeed.**
- **Don't forget to complete the compare and contrast worksheet on the next page.**

Compare	Contrast

TRUTH TWO: It isn't Free

I don't care what ad you've seen on social media promising Free Marketing, or "Launching your book to best-seller status at no cost!" It's a lie. It's all a lie. I'm sorry they lied to you and broke your heart, giving you high hopes for something that is in no way realistic. So grab a cup, collect your tears, and drink them down, because you were dooped. The truth about book marketing is this:

- ➢ You need to build a marketing budget (even a small one)
- ➢ You need Paid ads on social media and Amazon
- ➢ Marketing, especially for a book launch will cost you TIME
- ➢ It may require an arm, a leg, and/or a virgin's sacrifice to achieve.

Ok, that last bullet point was a joke. (Or was it? Only time will tell.) However, it can damned sure feel like it will take a prayer and a sacrifice to the publishing gods to get it done in a profitable manner.

TIP: When you are begging yourself for a 30 minute power nap, you will know that you are doing it right.

The most well-known fact in any business, (let's face it, Indie publishing is a business) is that you have to speed money to make money. After all, the title of this book is "Marketing on a Budget."

You need to build a budget

The first thing I had to do when determining my budget was to sit down and go over all of my finances. Before I did this, I said to myself, "Hell, I know there isn't any money left at the end of each week, especially with only one income in the household." I bet that sounds extremely familiar doesn't it?

Still, I needed to know if there happened to be some mystery hiding in the deep abyss of my finances, or in this case, my purse. I found pocket change in the bottom of my purse, the console of my car, the cup holder, behind the nightstands, on the nightstands, and even under the car seats.

Now to be fair, I only found about $1.27, but I took my $1.27, and drove to the local dollar store to purchase a planner. The planner cost me $1.07. I had .20 left, and I started to throw that shit right back into the cup holder of my car, but I stopped myself. *There is 20 cents toward my marketing budget right here.* Instead, I placed the two dimes in my wallet, and drove back home. After all, I was an author on a mission.

I have to note here that I absolutely despise pocket change. As you have probably gathered from the preceding paragraphs, I literally throw it everywhere. I never think about it unless I am out somewhere and decide I want a fountain Pepsi or something. Still, I finally saw a use for these coins that were long forgotten. I took it home and placed it in a trinket box that from that day forth, became my budget box. Change would go into it, and never be touched.

I apologize for leaving the topic of the planner, which is actually the main focus of this section. Shall we continue?

I sat down with my planner, and my laptop. I began documenting our household bills, organizing them by what was due weekly, and monthly. I added everything up and subtracted that from the weekly income.

I was surprised to find that we should have a significantly larger amount of money left over each week that what we actually had, even though we are both smokers. I opened out banking app, and we had maybe 19 cents left the day before pay day. "Where the hell did it all go?" I questioned. So what did I do, I started scrolling through the transaction records. Now, I can't tell you verbatim what I saw, but it went something like this:

13.19 McDonalds
 9.99 HBO subscription
 9.99 Showtime subscription
 3.99 online game purchase
15.99 online game purchase

There were probably 12 transactions at my favorite coffee spot as well. No wonder there were no extra funds in our account for me to even begin building a marketing budget. Don't get me wrong, 12.99 a month for Amazon Prime isn't bad. However, when you don't watch anything on the app, use the music, and barely, if ever shop online, it's kind of wasteful to keep the subscription.

I bet you can guess what I did next. I went through and started cancelling subscriptions. If I didn't use it, and my husband didn't use it, it didn't stay. I also deleted those games from my cellphone that I was purchasing coin packs for. I didn't have time to play games anyway. I had a book biz to build up. Those fast food transactions became one for $20.00 for pizza night for the family.

<u>Tip: I did make a note of when those unnecessary subscriptions were scheduled to renew. That</u>

<u>became the dates that my marketing account received a payment.</u>

One would be amazed at the amount of money the already have at their disposal. They simply have to find it. Remember, you are planning months in advance, so saving is necessary. Building your budget long before it's actually time to use it is a great move to make, and you will thank yourself for it later. Plan accordingly, and your book launch will love you.

You will Need Paid Ads

The biggest part of a successful book launch is getting your book out there. The best way to do that is through paid ads. If you haven't done so already now would be a good time to set up your Facebook author page. Remember to set this up as a business page. You'll also want to set up your Instagram business account, as well as add the Business Suite app, as it allows you to manage both your Facebook business account and your Instagram business account at this same time. This means when you make opposed for one, your post will go on both platforms. This is a really helpful tool when it comes to paid ads. For example: if your ad budget is fifty dollars, you will reach two platforms for the price of one.

Now would also be a great time to set up your Amazon author page with author central. This is a free feature offered by Amazon. Even though you're paid ads are set up through your kindle direct publishing account, your Amazon author page is a great link to use in your promo ads. You will want Amazon to count your downloads, and sales, and having your Amazon Author page set up will make it easier for that to happen. So, what is the recommended marketing budget for paid ads? I devote $100.00 for five days of paid ads. P.S. this is just for Facebook ads.

TIP: Amazon has two amazing guides to help you get the best ads created for the best chance at generating sales. Also, Amazon's campaign Advertising is simple to set up. Pick your budget!

TIP: When setting up Amazon ads, choose Dynamic bids. This will make your budget go farther. Recommended budget for Amazon ads is also $100.00.

In short, I recommend a $200.00 marketing ad budget; $100.00 for each platform. If you have a little extra to invest, look into Twitter ads. I personally haven't because I don't use Twitter much, but it is on my "To Do" list.

Indie Marketing for a Launch will cost TIME!

While the dollars are crucial for a successful book launch, they are mere crumbs when compared to the time you must invest in your launch. Now, I don't have to tell you much about the time that you must spend in this section because, I have shared a lot with you already. Any future tasks needed for your launch will be listed in the launch section.

TIP: Now would be a great time to make sure that your final draft is polished to perfection. The last thing that you need to be doing while planning a launch is writing, proofreading, or editing your manuscript. Make sure it's ready, and tucked away safely on your PC, with a backup or two for good measure.

Truth Three: You Need a Platform

I highly recommend a website, specifically for blogging. I know, I know, you're probably thinking, "She's telling me to do all this other shit, and now she wants me to start a blog?!?!"

Hear me out before you get too bent out of shape about this. I promise this is not a hard pill to swallow.

First, you can get a website free through WordPress or other platforms. So, this won't cost you anything. Sure, they will try to pimp their paid packages to you, but for now, it's only there for information.

Second, You're an indie author, and obviously not a famous one yet, so when people start seeing your name on social media, whether it be a post, a comment, or a book cover, their first question is "Who the hell is that?" A blogging website, along with an amazon author page will answer that question for your prospective reader. In short, it gives your future readers a chance to get to know you, the author.

While I will spend this book preaching to you about time, and how much of that specific valuable currency you will spend in launching your own book, I will also give you things to help you save time. This check list is one of those things.

Author Website Checklist

- Choose an easy to remember name for your website. (Mine is AbernathyBooks.com) Yours will look something like indieauthorsname@wordpress.com. There is a fee to drop the "WordPress" but it is not a necessary step for you to do right now.
- Write an "About the Author," which is a short autobiography, telling your readers who you are, where you're from, what you write, how long you have been writing, what your goals and dreams are, etc. Guess what, this is your first blog post.
- Second, write a blog post with your book cover and synopsis. Be sure to let the reader know when your books will release
- A third blog post could be a sneak peek into your book. I usually post my prologue, or a

short portion of my first chapter, like a teaser.
- Invite readers to follow you on your various social media platforms. (I have provided a script for this.)
- Be sure to include a photo of yourself. In your "about" section or blog post.

Invite Script

I love to engage with my readers; those who support me now, as well as those new to my work. Thank you for considering adding my books to your bookshelf. Follow me on these social media platforms, and tell me what you want to see.

Facebook: www.Facebook.com/AbernathyBooks

Twitter: @AbernathyBooks

Instagram: @AbernathyBooks

I can't wait to hear from you!

I know that I said it once, but I will say it again; if you do not have at least three social media platforms, get them, and get them fast. You will need them when it comes to marketing your launch because you can't rely on paid ads alone to build the traffic to your book. Your social media accounts, combined with your author's website, creates your author platform.

Part Two: Launching your Book

CONGRATULATIONS! You have made it through part one of this book, hopefully unscathed. Since you are at this point, that can only mean one of two things:

1.) You read through part one, and followed all the steps, or
2.) You skipped to part two just to get to the launch process.

If you did the second thing, I feel bad for your brain later when it's absolutely fried worse than a turkey on Thanksgiving because you have no idea what I am talking about moving forward. It's kind of like cutting in line at an amusement park; you're ready to experience the ride, but you missed the instructions on what to expect. Sure, you **MIGHT** survive, but there may be bald spots just above your temples where you pulled your hair out.

If you did the first thing, then sit back. It won't be a breeze, but you are well prepared for what is coming, and you will end the ride with all of your hair still intact though, it may be just a bit disheveled. Therefore, without further ado, let us proceed with launch prep.

New Book Launch Procedures Q&A

- **When does this begin?** Technically, the day of "live" on Amazon for kindle editions, however, you will want to schedule your official launch to begin 10 days after your book goes live.
- **What needs to be in place in time for the book launch?**

1.) You will need at least 20 people to commit to purchasing on "live" day.
2.) You will need each of those people to read 2-4 chapters of the book, and post a

review on Amazon within 5 days of purchase.

3.) You will need press release written and ready to go out the day before official launch.

➢ <u>**What are the goals of this Procedure?**</u>

    1.) Gain Exposure

    2.) Build a following

    3.) Market a new Title

    4.) Reach Best Seller Status

    5.) This will also be a light launch for the paperback edition, and preparing for the official paperback launch promotion to begin on day three of the kindle launch.

I can already feel your heart racing after reading through the Q & A. You may even be yelling into the universe that I never said anything about 20 committed buyers on the day your book is live on Amazon. You're right, I didn't. However, take a deep breath and think. We are just planning right now. Also remember, in the disclaimer, I advised reading this book in its entirety before ever planning a launch? You always study before a test, right?

Now, let's address where those twenty committed buyers are going to come from. To do that, let me ask you a few questions:

1.) Did you ever share on social media that you were publishing a book?
2.) Did you work on building your whole author platform?
3.) Did you pay attention to the likes, comments, and other engagements that came from those social media posts?

If you answered "yes" to all three of those questions, then those twenty people are out there in social media land. All you have to do is find them. Keep in mind that Amazon is extremely picky about reviews, so keep close family and friends that are on your friends list out of the criteria as far as reviews are concerned. Now, the sales will help during the official launch of course, but right now, we want to focus on those people that Amazon would be least likely to boot off.

Therefore, this is where you are going to step into the world of direct sales and network marketing. Think of every member of every group you are in as a contact. You have probably even made friends with other indie authors through your platforms, and they are the perfect group to reach out to, but don't single out anyone. Some of the reviews may get by Amazon's algorithm.

Send messages through your social media lists through messenger, text messages, your email contacts telling everyone how much you need their support. (Be sure to use the word "support" instead of "help" as it triggers a different psychological response.) In this message, there are some key points that you do not want to miss when reaching out to this list of people. You will want to be sure to tell them that:

    1.) The release date is (specific date)
    2.) The book will be $0.99
    3.) You need a purchase
    4.) You need a review.

While Amazon frowns upon paid reviews, I do tell these people that once their review posts, I will refund their .99 plus tax via PayPal. To me, these are media copies of a book that the big publishing houses send out to the reviewers like New York Times Best Seller List, and other review platforms. Audible gives away promo codes to authors and narrators for review copies, and those reviews often stay on the site, so at this point, I see no difference.

Also, be sure to state that you need HONEST reviews. No author gets only five star reviews, and that includes the big name guys and gals. You are an Indie author. If Stephen King or Stephanie Meyer can get negative reviews, so can you. So while this method is frowned upon, we also want it to be as ethical as possible. Below, I have provided the message that I send to my list of committed buyers as an "example"

Dear Reader/Reviewer,

If you had the chance to make a difference in someone's life, and that support only cost you one .99 investment, would you do it? If you answered yes to my question, then let me tell you what I need:

- *I have a new book launching very soon, and I need 20 people to commit to purchasing that book, in the kindle version, from Amazon within the first five days of it going "live."*
- *Read the first two to four sections/chapters, and write an HONEST REVIEW of the book, based on what you have read within five days of that purchase.*
- *Once your review posts to Amazon, I will refund your $0.99 plus tax via PayPal immediately.*
- *I need all reviews within 10 days after the live date, because on day 11, I will officially launch my book.*
- *As an extra thank you, I will email you a promo code to receive a paperback copy of*

any of my books at my cost, plus shipping and handling.
- *Please let me know as soon as possible if you can commit to supporting me on my journey to the Amazon's best seller list.*

Sincerely,

Author Dianah Brock.

Now, don't get discouraged when people don't answer you right away, but also stay vigilant of those replies. Also, the reality is, it may not happen. I have built up a list of reviewers through my audiobooks, and established a great list, but that took a lot of time to do. As a perk, when the time comes for you to attempt this launch procedure, shoot me an email of a message through my Facebook page. I will commit to supporting you ☺ and you won't have to reimburse me through PayPal.

Now, let's move on to that procedure…after I take a cigarette break. Don't judge.

New Book Title Launch Procedure

Preparing

- Schedule new book launch for 10 days after the official "Live" date for kindle on Amazon.com
- Notify review team that the book is "Live" and give 48 hours to purchase the book @ $0.99. *NOTE* this email is just a heads up notice that you have the title going live within the next five days. If your committed buyers/review team are following you on Amazon, they will be notified again by them.
- Set book cost at the lowest price of .99. Leave the book at .99 for 3 to 5 days, then raise the price to 9.99.
- The day after the price increase, schedule a 5 day free promotion for the Official launch date.
- Check the KDP dashboard daily for sales (Looking for those reviewer purchases)
- Verify review to the reviewer as they come in and make good on your reimbursement promise.
- Once there are three reviews, write the first press release, and include those three reviews. The first press release should be

sent out the day before your official launch date.

> **The Indie Author's No Bullshit Guide to Marketing on a Budget will be free to download Tomorrow (Date)**
>
> Ava Abernathy, a twelve time published independent author of fictional suspense thrillers (pseudonym Dianah Brock) is proud to present her first ever non-fiction, self-help book, "The Indie Author's No Bullshit Guide to Marketing on a Budget"
>
> Ava Knows the struggle of Marketing that all independently published authors endure day in and day out. After many experiments with trial and error, she decided to compile that strategy into a book to help other independent authors like herself find more success in this highly competitive industry.
>
> Ava Abernathy's (hyperlinked title) will be available for free download on Amazon for 5 days (from-to) at (insert book link). The Indie Author's Guide is rated (give rating from those reviews) by those who have purchased the book. Here is what they had to say:
>
> Review one
> Review two
> Review three (if available)
>
> For more information, questions, or to schedule an interview about the press release, please contact Ava through her contact us section of her website at www.AbernathyBooks.com

Writing a press release can seem intimidating. God knows I was terrified to even give it a shot. Not to mention my limited computer skills meant I had to learn how to Hyper link, and a lot of other details. Still, I pulled it off, and I believe that you can too. After all, you're a bad ass independently published author right?

So, why was it necessary for you to learn to write a press release? Well, of course I'm going to answer that.

Where exactly am I going to send this? I'm going to answer that too. But first, I have some questions for you.

- Did you research groups, bloggers, vloggers, and such on social media?
- Did you research local news stations, radio stations, and podcasts?
- Did you make your list?

If you answered yes to these questions, then you've answered the questions you've asked of me already.

Question one: *Why was it necessary for you to learn how to write a press release?*
Answer one: *You just wrote a catchy ad that will be sent all over social media. Make this your paid ad for two days.*
Question two: *Where exactly am I going to send the press release?*

Answer two: *EVERYWHERE!!* *That entire list that you created will receive this press release, not to mention everyone you reach with your paid ads. The key to this is not to rely on the paid ads alone. SHARE! SHARE! SHARE!*

Didn't know about this research and list? Maybe you shouldn't have been a cheater, cheater, pumpkin eater and skipped part one.

Now, on to the next checklist.

"Wait, why are we getting the full five day checklist at once instead of day by day?" Well my fellow indie author, allow me to answer that question.

1. I don't want you to have any surprises.
2. If you know what is coming, then you may adapt this to fit your abilities, accesses, or make any variations in planning that you see fit.
3. Only day one really needs the extra attention. Therefore, I will repeat myself at the end of this section, and I will do so because you have a lot of work to do.
4. I don't want you to forget anything. Think about it; your success with this process is also my success. Your failure is my failure.

Five Day Book Launch Checklist

Day One:

- Ensure paid ad is Live (2 day ad)
- Post to all social media platforms
- Send email to subscribers (press release)
- Publish press release to website as a blog

Day Two:

- Check your book's rating on Amazon to see if you have reached best seller status. If you did, then you will want the second press release ready stating so. If not, then your press release will read the same as the first, only it will state that there are only three days left in the free promo.
- Check your social media stats to see how far your reach is going. You should be growing

in page followers, or at least be getting engagements from your posts.
- Post to all social media platforms (this also includes all the groups just like on day one.)
- Check your Amazon rating for your book again. If you have not met best seller status, then the press release that you prepared will be what you begin to share on day three.
- Send the day three press release to your media list
- Schedule your next 2 day ad for Facebook & Instagram.

Day Three:

- Ensure day three paid ad is live (2 days)
- Post to all social media platforms
- Send email reminder to subscribers of your website (if you have that option.)
- Verify Press release receipt to media outlets

- At the end of the day, check sales stats on KDP. *How are your sales? Did you reach Best Seller status on Amazon? What is your book's ranking in the genre (Self-help & Non-Fiction)*

IMPORTANT: If you have not reached best seller status by day three, DON'T PANIC YET!!

Day Four: On day four, before beginning your tasks for the day, check to see if you have reached Best Seller Status. If you did, congratulations. If not, don't sweat it. Those free downloads should be speaking for your book, and we will be checking again.

- Share on all social media platforms
- Check your stats for your paid ads.
- At 7:00 p.m. check your stats again. You will want to record your sales total, your

ranking on Amazon, and see if you have reached the Best Seller's list.

GOAL: By 7:00 p.m. you title should be at "Best Seller." If it is, CONGRATULATIONS!!!

If you have reached "Best Seller" status, do the following:

- Email day five press release to media outlets stating that your book has made it to best seller. Don't worry, I have included Day 3 and two scenarios for Day 5 Press Releases a little farther into this book.
- Smile, pat yourself on the back, and cry, because you just crushed another goal in your career as an independent author. You are now a **BEST SELLING AUTHOR!**

If you did NOT reach best seller status, have no fear. A lot of downloads have gone out, so use the press release for scenario two provided in this book at the end of this section.

Day Five

- Check & verify your paid ad is live (2 days)
- Post last day ad to all social media platforms. Remember to include the press release with scenario one.
- Last day reminder email to subscribers of your website (if you have this option)
- Post press release to the website as a blog.
- About 7:00 pm EST, go into your KDP dashboard, end the promo early, and set your book price at $2.99 and that paperback that you dropped to the lowest price Amazon would allow, raise that price to normal.

Once you have completed all of these tasks, take the rest of the day to relax. Let your book do its thing.

Just remember, through the course of this promotion, you will want to do the following:

- ➢ Make sure you are engaging with people on social media that may be commenting on your posts, ads, etc.
- ➢ Check your emails at the end of the day. There is a high probability that you have interview requests, other reviews, or praises from other Indie Authors that you can use later to continue to boost your following and promote your book.

Beware of scammers, or anyone that wants you to pay for the interview. It doesn't work that way. You are a best-selling author. If anyone is getting paid it's you, but interviews should honestly be done free. Remember to be humble and show integrity in your author biz. Just because you are a best seller doesn't mean you are Stephen King. You ain't got it like that yet homie.

THIS HAS TO BE SAID HERE, NOW

I am not now, nor have I ever promised you that you would make the Amazon Best Sellers List. I am simply telling you that:

1.) It's a goal that we were reaching for.
2.) It is possible that it can happen with a proper launch.
3.) Just because it works for some, doesn't mean it will work for all. No Bullshit guide, remember?

Now that we have cleared that I have said that, let's continue on to your checklists and resources for your launch. Remember I asked that you read this book in its entirety before planning anything. I am hoping this is at least your second read through, and that you are planning things.

Day before Launch Checklist

- Look for all of your reviews for the title.
- Email those reviewers who have not posted their reviews to Amazon. Remind them they only need to review 2 to 4 chapters.
- Send the press release out a second time in the evening, just in case.
- Schedule your paid ads for Facebook i.e. your press release for days one and two.
- Schedule your paid ads for days three and four *(Wait? Say what!?!?!)*
- Schedule your day five press release with the headline "Last day to grab this Amazon Number One best seller Absolutely Free! (Your book should have made the best seller's list by now)
- Announce the launch on all of your social media sites every single day, in every single place. Remember that high cost in time we

talked about? This is where it comes from. Yes, you paid for ads, but work with them to get even farther with your reach.

REMEMBER: When writing press releases, you also have a paperback edition available. It wouldn't be a bad idea to mention this as well as the price. It could grab you some sales, like authentic sales of your paperback edition during your Kindle launch. If not, the price is out there, and that will grab attention when we launch your paperback because, oh yeah, we are going to do that too.

New Title Book Launch Day One

Good Morning! It's launch day! Grab a cup of coffee, a shot of vodka, and settle in for one hell of a long day. If you have prepped as you should have, your ads are running this morning, so the exposure for your new book, and you as an author is already happening. So settle in at your computer and get ready because you have a lot of work to do today.

Begin with social media platforms. If you have a website that you have actually paid for, this will be a breeze. If not, then it's going to take some time.

We are going to begin with the most active, and time consuming platform first: Facebook.

Facebook Checklist

- Announce free promo on your personal page. (Keep in mind, this reach won't be much, so don't count on it. You just never know)
- Announce free promo on your official Facebook author page. If you have installed Facebook Business Suite, and linked your Instagram account, you will be making two posts from one location and this will save you some time.
- Announce your free promo in your reader's group if you have one.

Now, this is where the fun begins. Remember all of those book groups you joined for indie authors, book lovers, etc. You are going to copy and paste your ad and go through each and every one of those groups and post your ad, aka press release. Be sure to include your book trailer, book cover photo, or both as it will help those interested find your book in the event Amazon is having a meltdown that day and the links don't work.

Other Platforms

- **Twitter- Keep** in mind, Twitter has a character limit. Therefore, I would recommend including the beginning of the press release, and then linking your Facebook page post so that interested people can continue to read.
- **Instagram:** If you installed Facebook Business Suite, then you are already posted here.
- **Website:** Did you include your press release on the home page of your website as a blog? If not, now is a great time for some quick copy, paste, and use your book cover as the image.

➢ **Email Subscribers-** Not all free platforms for websites allow you to have subscribers. So, if you have one that didn't give the option, don't worry here. However, if you pay for your website, then definitely email those subscribers on day one. Don't count on Amazon do their job and notify your followers of the drop in price for your book.

IMPORTANT: DO NOT CHECK YOUR KDP SALES DASHBOARD ON DAY ONE! YOU WILL DRIVE YOURSELF CRAZY. ON DAY ONE OF THE PROMO, YOUR DASHBOARD DOES NOT EXIST!!!

Repeat Social Media Posting again in the evening as well. You want those posts to stay visible as much as possible. Sure, you have paid ads interrupting other videos and coming up in the news feed of the audience that you selected, but that isn't enough. Also, be sure to reply to comments, questions, messages you receive through your social media platforms. Engaging with potential readers allows you to get closer to the sale, or in this case, the free download of your book from Amazon. It has been my personal experience that I am more likely to purchase a book written by an Indie Author if they engage with their audience, so I highly recommend the same.

Day Three Press Release (will run as two-day ad)

The Indie Author's No Bullshit Guide to Marketing on a Budget is Gaining Momentum!

Ava Abernathy, a twelve time independently published author of fictional suspense thrillers, with a dash of romance, released her first ever, non-fiction, self-help book absolutely free two days ago. The promotion is set to expire on, (give date and time) so grab it while the promotion is live. There are only three days left!

Ava knows the struggle of Marketing that all independent authors go through. Fighting to rise up through the ranks of those Amazon sales numbers. With (# of copies sold) already claimed in the first 48 hours, the book is definitely gaining momentum.
Abernathy's (hyperlinked book title) is only available for free download for three more days. With its current amazon rating of (Amazon rating here), this just may be that secret weapon indie authors are looking for. Here is what readers have to say:

(Include 2-3 Reviews here)

For more information, questions, or to schedule an interview with the author, use the "Contact us" tab on Ava's website at www.AbernathyBooks.com

Day Five Press Release (run for 2 days)

(Scenario one)

The Indie Author's No Bullshit Guide to marketing on a Budget Now a Best Seller!

Four days ago, Ava Abernathy, a twelve time independently published fictional author released her first ever non-fiction, self-help book for struggling independent authors, just like herself. In those four short days, this book has quickly climbed the ranks of Amazon, becoming a best seller, with (#) copies downloaded 100% free of charge.

Here is what readers are saying:

(Post two to three reviews here)

Today is the last day to grab this book, absolutely free! Go to AbernathyBooks.com, click download, and you will be redirected to Amazon to claim your free copy. Independent authors who are eager to make a profit from their writing need to grab this book before the promotion is over. If you miss the deadline, don't worry, Ava is leaving the book at a discounted price of only .99 for a short time. Judging by the reviews, it's well worth the .99 price tag.

For more information, questions, or to schedule an interview regarding the book, please visit www.AbernathyBooks.com contact page and submit your request.

Day Five Press Release (Scenario 2)

The Indie Author's No Bullshit Guide to Marketing on a Budget Free Promotion ends tonight!

Four days ago, Ava Abernathy, a twelve time independently published author of fictional suspense thrillers went out on a limb, and released her first ever non-fiction, self-help book for Independent authors just like herself. She wanted to help other indie writers have a better chance of fighting the marketing struggle involved in this highly demanding and competitive industry.

Here is what she has accomplished in just four short days!

_____ downloads

_____ Ranking on Amazon

*Any other results your feel would be beneficial to promoting your promotion.

Here is what readers have to say: (2-3 reviews)

Today is the last day to grab this increasingly popular book absolutely free on Kindle. The deadline is Midnight. However, if you miss that deadline, Ava will leave the book available for only .99 for a limited time.

For more information, questions, or to schedule an interview with the author, visit the contact us section of her website.

The Day After the promo ends

You have accomplished a lot in five days. Now, its day six. Pull up your stats, take a look at what you have accomplished. How do you feel about your progress through this process? Do some free writing about your thoughts and feelings.

_____
_____
_____
_____
_____
_____
_____
_____
_____
_____
_____
_____
_____
_____
_____
_____
_____
_____
_____
_____
_____
_____

Conclusion of Kindle New Title Launch

So, let's recap:

- At this point, you have finished your book, published, and used Amazon's free promotion to hit best seller, or at least, you came pretty damn close. Regardless of best seller status or not, your stats on KDP should be looking pretty good on your dashboard. You have also gained exposure, introduced your book to the world, built your following, and possibly even gained some actual sales as well from your paperback edition.
- The five day Kindle Launch Promo also acted as a soft launch for your paperback edition of your book. Therefore, you have already set the course for paperback sales. With all of your marketing in these past five days, with only one

mention of your paperback edition, you have caught the interest of those readers that prefer to hold a physical book in their hands.

- Even if you didn't gain any paperback sales, there is no point in stressing it right now. Like I said, you caught some attention of those paperback fans. Besides, Prospective buyers have at least visited your title's listing on Amazon, checked on that "over-priced" paperback edition and thought to themselves, "If only it were cheaper." What they don't know is, you are about to make that private thought a reality.

Part Three: Paperback Launch

Introduction

At this point, you have had a successful online presence for the new book, your brand, and most importantly, yourself. You have gained a lot of sales, free downloads, and hit the best seller's list on Amazon. (Hopefully) You may be thinking, "What does the kindle edition have to do with the paperback edition?" You may even be wondering why you should even care about your paperback edition.

The truth is, paperbacks, or print copies are still very desirable in the literary world. Using the momentum that you have gained to draw attention to your kindle edition can do a few things for your paperback version.

It can:

- Reach those potential buyers that followed your link on social media, looking for the price and/or availability of your book in paperback format.
- As you go through the next five days of marketing the paperback edition, you are reminding all of those who either purchased or considered your book that it's there, and still growing. It isn't some fad that is going to go away any time soon.
- All of those media outlets that you sent press releases to be seeing that you are not going away as well, and maybe there is something to this author that makes them stand out from the rest.
- If the media outlets didn't run your press release, but you are still there in the spotlight after the free promotion is over,

they are probably kicking themselves in the ass for not running that press release, especially when they realized that they could have shared some positive news in a time when most of what we see and hear in the media is always negative. Oh what a breath of fresh air that press release could have been.

- ❖ You have also caught the attention of Audiobook fans who are already "following" you on Amazon, Facebook, or one of your other platforms because you are literally everywhere. They want this book too, but they don't have the time to sit down and read, so they listen on their commute to work, or during their downtime in their offices, or on lunch breaks. They are watching and waiting for that audiobook to come out.

In addition to showing the world of readers that you are indeed reaching out to everyone, no matter what format they choose to get their literary fix, you are also going to make more on sales, and you aren't simply marketing a free digital book, and catering to the digital readers. You are an author for all.

All of this can mean more income for your hard work, which is one of the reasons you published in the first place. Besides, you would really like a return on the investment into all of those paid ads right? Now, let's talk about that less vigorous, more profitable promotion of your paperback or print edition.

Five Day Paperback Launch Pre-plan

On day one after your promotion ended, you were supposed to rest up. Some will, but if you are anything like me, you didn't do that. Your mind began to run away with you and you started tweaking the program to work for your better, analyzing your ad results, or something. You did anything but rest.

Day two after the end of your kindle promotion is the official prep day for that paperback that had a minimum price of say 9.99. However, you have studied indie publishing and this book so well, you listed that book for 15.99. The time has come for you to take advantage of that absolute minimum price option for five days. Remember, if someone is "following" you on Amazon, they will get a notification of this price drop. You have the potential for sales before the launch even happens. (We are optimistic after all.☺)

So, here is how we prepare for this launch, and my apologies, you don't get a real break yet. (It's coming, I promise.)

The first thing we are going to do, is pre-write the press release. We need to make it a little different for a few reasons:

    1.) You aren't giving your book away
    2.) It is a print version
    3.) There will be a massive price drop

Of course, I have provided you with a sample of the press release, which will double as your five day paid ad for Facebook and Instagram. Next page please!

The Indie Author's No Bullshit Guide to Marketing on a Budget is the newest tool for independently published authors competing to make their mark in the literary world.

Written by independent fiction author Ava Abernathy AKA Dianah Brock, the kindle edition of this book has sold (number of copies) since its official launch on (Date of launch), its ranked ____ on Amazon, and the reviewers are raving!

(Insert two to three five star reviews here)

Refusing to allow authors to continue to struggle through the jungle of marketing, and wasting precious time and money on books and other long form sales pitches, Abernathy sat down and converted her strategy into book format to help support other indie authors just like her.

Right now, for all of you paperback lovers out there, "The Indie Author's No Bullshit Guide to Marketing on a Budget" has dropped to the lowest price Amazon will allow, 9.99. That's literally the absolute lowest price in paperback format. However, this price drop won't last for long, so follow the link and claim your copy today!

For more information, questions, or to schedule an interview with the author, please visit the "Contact Us" tab on the official website, www.AbernathyBooks.com

Now that you have written your totally epic press release that will double as your five day ad, it's time to get that sucker scheduled. I recommend a budget of $50.00 for this ad to run for five days. Read through your press release/ad and make sure that you have included the following information:

- Your Amazon star and numerical rating
- 2-3 of your best reviews
- Informed your potential buyers that this is a limited time offer.

You will also want to make sure that you have advertised your special offer on your website. If you have paid for a website that allows email marketing, now is a good time to schedule an email campaign to be sent via email to your subscribers. For your home page ad on your official website, be sure to include the following:

- ❖ Link to Amazon author page for follows
- ❖ Your Amazon rating (Star and numerical)
- ❖ Reviews
- ❖ Reminder to subscribe to your newsletter, and confirm subscription in the email they receive. *(This is for newcomers who are just checking you out, and happen to like what they see.)*

TIP: I offer a free bookmark to the first 20 people who subscribe to my newsletter, and include all of their information.

I know that you may be ready to pull your hair out, and may even be looking in the mirror screaming, "When does this job ever END?" Even worse, you may be standing outside in the darkness looking up at the moon, screaming WHY at the top of your lungs to the Gods of the literary universe, and questioning if a virgin's sacrifice may indeed be required to complete all of these tasks. Don't worry.

It's all worth it; except for the virgin's sacrifice. That is not recommended, is definitely illegal, and this isn't *Achievement by Possession*. (Check out my website for more information on the aforementioned book title☺)

Now, prep continued…

Create a word document (or google doc if that is your preference) for your social media posts. You can use your press release if you want, but statistics show that social media users engage more with photos and videos than they do with plain text. Remember, copy and paste is your best friend in the marketing world. Do not forget to include a call to action in this post; something like, "Visit my website for more information" or "Follow me on Amazon for updates."

Next, you will want to schedule your announcement post for your Facebook author page, and Instagram account. Remember, if you purchased a website, you can manage social media posts from one spot, or use Facebook Business Suite to post to both platforms at once. I would recommend scheduling the announcement to post once a day for five days. This will save you some valuable time, especially when it comes to going through all of the groups you have joined on Facebook and posting over and over again.

If you have created a Facebook Group of your own, be sure to schedule your post there as well, but do this only once, and pin it to the top of the page so it's the first thing visitors see when they visit your group. Now that you have pre-written everything, and ads and posts are scheduled, let's jump right into day one of the five day paperback launch.

Five Day Paperback Launch
Day One

You will begin day one of this launch the same way you did with the kindle edition. You will begin with social media platforms. Keep in mind that this does not mean your personal Facebook group or business page. Those are already scheduled, as well as your ads.

- ❖ First, verify that your paid ad is up and running. After that, the real work begins.
- ❖ Post your launch announcement (press release) on your own Facebook profile.
- ❖ Go through your individual groups, and copy and paste your press release there. The hyperlinks should post a preview of your Amazon page.
- ❖ **Post to twitter**. Keep in mind that Tweets have a character limit, so take your headline, and use that as your tweet, followed by the

link to your press release that you posted on your blog or website the day before. This also means more traffic to your blog site as well, which can be a good thing, especially if you have added blogs about writing or sneak peeks of your books. You may grab a reader that way.

- ❖ **Post to Instagram** with a cover of your book. Remember, hashtags are your friend on Insta, so use them all. A list of recommended hashtags can be found in the back of this books under the useful information guide.
- ❖ **Post to SnapChat.** If this is a platform you use, I would recommend ordering a copy of your book at some point before the launch, so you can hold the physical copy in your hands. That would make a great Snap announcement, a photo of you holding your

book, showing as much excitement as you can.

- ❖ **Post to LinkedIn.** If you use this platform, it is a great place to also post your info. You never know if there are literary agents or publishing houses looking for the next great writer, or a movie producer looking for that next great series. LinkedIn is full of Professionals. Give it a shot. What could it hurt?

!!!IMPORTANT!!!

DO NOT RESEND EMAILS TO WEBSITE SUBSCRIBERS!!! IT LOOKS SPAMMY, AND YOU COULD LOSE MORE THAN YOU GAIN!!!

DO: Check your email at the end of the day so you can stay on top of those new subscribers, and those free bookmarks (in my case. Not required.)

DON'T: Check your KDP dashboard for sales. If you get discouraged on day one, it tends to reflect in your words and posts to social media. You do not want any friends, family, or followers to "Feel the vibes" of discouragement. You also don't want pity engagements either. Both are unprofessional and unflattering.

REMEMBER the power of the spoken (or written) word is real. Think positive. Speak positive. Write positive. Post positive. BELIEVE POSITIVE!!

Five Day Paperback Launch

Day Two

- ❖ Make your social media posts, just as you did the day before, starting with Facebook groups, and moving forward.
- ❖ Check your Blog/Website for new subscribers. Take the time to create a heartfelt thank you/welcome email. If you have the finances to show your appreciation, even as a small gesture, request the mailing address for the first 20 people who subscribe, and send them a personally written thank you card in the mail. I send bookmarks and a card, but you get the idea. Appreciation is key here.
- ❖ If you choose to offer a free "thank you" gift to new subscribers, please be sure to include in your email that: You will never sell or

share their information, and you promise to never fill their mailboxes with junk mail.
- ❖ Re-send your press release to your media outlets. Be sure to edit that the limited time discount ends in three days.

TIP If you have a particular contact @ a media outlet, and it is financially possible, offer a free copy of your book to them as a thank you for sharing your press release. It helps to make friends in this biz.

Five Day Paperback Launch

Day Three

Day three is another day of repetition that will ensure that you need coffee, and if you live in a state where it's legal, probably a joint for good measure. (Joke☺) Honestly though, a shot of Malibu in your coffee couldn't hurt.

- ❖ Daily social media posts. This time, be sure to announce that there are only two days left to get your paperback at this discounted rate before the price goes up. Don't forget to post this to all of your social media platforms. You know the drill by now.
- ❖ Check emails
- ❖ Check website for new subscribers (Don't get discouraged if there aren't any new ones.)

- Finally, check the stats of your paid ads on Facebook. I know that within three days, Facebook has tempted you to see this by notifying you that "Your ad is performing well" but don't fall for it until now. It's day three; check that shit.
- Finally, FINALLY, check your KDP dashboard for sales. Anything sold in the past two days should be showing up now.
- Pop over and check out your stats on Amazon. Has your book ranking went up? Has your star rating changed? If it has, and its positive results, a mid-day social media post on your page and your personal Facebook profile isn't a bad idea at all! Share the news with a screenshot, and don't forget to share how excited and blessed you are with your book's performance. A humble author is an admired author. Be sure

to include a thank you in that post as well, for good measure.

❖ Remember to interact with commenters on social media, answer relevant messages and emails, and keep sending those thank you/welcome emails to your new subscribers.

❖ Keep in mind that on the Facebook platform, you have the option to mention people who react to posts but don't comment. Use this feature as a way to get them to engage more, even if it's a simple thank you. If there is one thing I have learned in this business, it is that the more valuable and appreciated you make people feel, the more they keep coming back to your page, your blog, your books.

Five Day Paperback Launch

Day Four

It's coming down to the wire now. This five day book launch has only two days left, (Day four and five) and is almost over. With Day four staring you in the face like a puppy that is begging for the steak from your plate, it's time to make the puppy, AKA day four work for the steak.

Therefore, we are going to mix it up a bit on how we preform our tasks for the day. Ok, we aren't going to mix it up; we are going to reverse the entire process because we have a lot of attention to grab, and only two more days to grab it. So, here we go.

- ❖ Check your KDP dashboard. Are there any new sales? If so, how many books did you sell?
- ❖ Check your book out on Amazon and look at the rating. Has it changed? Has your star

rating changed? Are there any new reviews, especially the positive ones? Has the number of follows gone up, and if so, by how much? Take a screenshot if there is a notable, and positive change.

- ❖ Make notes of the numbers and data from KDP and Amazon. We will use it later.
- ❖ Check your Facebook ad stats. How is it preforming? Do you feel that the reach of your paid ad is sufficient to your goals for this five day launch? Most importantly, does your budget allow for a $25.00 boost? (If not, that's ok, we are just going to have to work harder, and that's all.)
- ❖ Check your blog/website. Do you have new subscribers? How many? Be sure to go ahead and send out those thank you/welcome emails for good measure so you don't forget.

❖ Make a note of how many new subscribers you have now as well.

Keep in mind that you do currently have a five day paid ad that is currently running on Facebook, so for now, that platform is covered. We are going to leave social media alone right now.

Instead of making social media posts our main focus at the moment, we are going to take some time and review the stats that you have recorded. If all of your analytics are positive, then we have something that we can use to really grab some attention for you and for your book.

Sit down, and use the data sheet to create an entirely new blog post. This blog post will serve as your social media post later on today. Sure, this new post is going to get a paid boost on Facebook, (if the money is in the budget. If not, don't worry) but it will also serve as the post for all social media outlets.

For instructional purposes, we are going to look at the data sheet, and use that to create a catchy new blog post that will make prospective readers think, "Maybe there really is something to this new author/book. Let me go check it out."

Now, let's go take a look at the data sheets. The first is blank for you to fill out. If you have the kindle edition, I recommend sitting down with a legal pad and recreating this document. If you have the print version, just write in the book. (I know, I know, it's evil as hell, but this is a workbook so its fine.) If you have the audio version, hit the pause button.

Amazon Portion of Data Sheet

Data Type	Reading	Increase or decrease
Paperback sales		
Kindle sales		
KU pages read		
Reviews		
Star rating		
Book ranking		

Now, take a look at your results. Are the numbers higher? If so, GREAT! Your launch is going well. If not, don't sweat it, the majority of book sales happen after a launch is over, and paperback sales are a lot harder to get than digital these days.

Still, there are lovers of paperbacks out there, and they are looking. And don't worry, your launch is still going well because you are reaching thousands of people on a daily basis, and letting them know that you and your book are out there. There is no such thing as a failed launch. Remember that; *"Failure to Launch"* was just a movie.

As an example, here is a data sheet that I have filled in with some fictional data. Notice I didn't go all out with high numbers where everything looks just perfect. It's unrealistic, and I believe truly dishonest to give people these high hopes or make promises that their numbers will look huge, and they became a celebrity author overnight. That is not the purpose of this book. No bullshit, Remember.

Amazon Portion of Data Sheet

Data Type	Reading	Increase or decrease
Paperback sales	12	Increase by 3
Kindle sales	8	Decrease by 3
KU pages read	254	Increase by 72
Reviews	2	Decrease by 7
Star rating	4.75	Increase from 4.50
Book ranking	9,926	Increase from 10,926
Total copies sold so far	583	Increase from 546

At first glance of the sample data sheet, it looks like we aren't doing that great. However, from a creative marketing side, I see the info I need to build one hell of a post that will do the following:

- Engage potential buyers
- Interest potential followers
- Most importantly, motivate myself to push hard in these last two days of my book launch to reach the goals I set before starting.

Remember, there is always a chance that this launch will not yield the results you want. I am not sure who said this, but it's my favorite quote:

"Shoot for the moon. Even if you miss, you will land among the stars."

1. If the copyright holder of this quote reads this, just know I am in no way claiming

credit for such a brilliant and inspirational quote.
2. Know that I would love to cite you, if I knew who you were.
3. Thank you for such an amazing and inspirational quote, as it has changed my entire life, and I wish nothing more than to share it with as many as possible.

Now, back to the data. If you look at the data sheet with a "glass half full" perspective, we have a great chance of grabbing a lot of attention. However, more information is needed before we can write that attention grabbing sales blog/post/press release. To get this data, we need to visit our Ad Manager on Facebook.™

Answer these questions (kindle and paperback ads)

*Remember, your other social media numbers are there as well.

1. How many people have you reached?

Paid ad _____
Unpaid_____
2. How many reactions has your ad received? _____
3. Are the reactions positive or negative? _____
4. How many clicks have you received? _____
5. How many shares? _____

Now, let's go to your Facebook ™ page.

1. How many "likes" does your page have? _____

2. Do you see an increase, decrease, or no change? _____

3. How many followers does your page have? _____

4. Do you see an increase, decrease, or no change? _____

Don't forget to visit your other social media sites and answer these same questions.

Be sure to record your answers. Also remember to document comments and messages as well. You will receive spam messages from people wanting you to pay them to promote your work. Just ignore those, or do what I do, and send them a buy link, with a request for an honest review. (Winky face)

Now that you have gathered all of the data from your social media accounts and Ad Manager/Business Suite, here is what you should see:

- An increase in reach for your paid ad.
- Generic reach should be increasing (if you're being a good soldier, and doing the work.)
- Reactions may be dropping. (This happens when the same people see your ad over and over again. It also means they are getting bored.

- Increase in clicks
- Increase in likes and follows for your page. One may be increasing more than the other. Some only follow the page, while others like it and move on.
- Shares may be increasing, but they are iffy. Shares happen in one of two scenarios. The first, depends on whether or not you have a supportive following. The second, whether or not your ad is "catchy." If you're getting shares, it is a good thing, of you aren't, it doesn't necessarily mean anything.

While we want to focus on the reach, engagements are our number one goal, with sales being number two.

- If your reach is high, but engagements and sales are low, that is when we want to revamp our marketing strategy. We need a real attention grabber.
- If our reach is high, and our engagements are high, but sales are low, we need something to make that potential buyer open their wallet.
- If reach is high, engagements are high, and sales are high, its smooth sailing from here on out, but why waste the momentum?

In short, you have day four and day five (two days) to "bring it home" with your paperback launch. Therefore, the next thing I am going to share with you will be a blog/press release/post for each of these three scenarios. You may adapt these however you like to fit the needs of you and your book, but don't copy it too much. That's frowned upon. ☹

Scenario one- Reach is high, engagements and sales are low.

> **"Two days left to buy the book that will change your Marketing game FOREVER!"**
>
> ***"The Indie Author's No Bullsh*t Guide to Marketing on a Budget"*** is the hottest new tool for Indie Authors. Sales are increasing by the day for this blunt, yet professionally written guide that shares all the truth about Indie Marketing.
>
> With almost 600 copies sold since its release on, (release date here for Kindle version) with a 4.75 star rating on Amazon, and a reach of over 5,000 people on social media through generic marketing alone, the Indie Writers are talking, and here is what they have to say:
>
> *Three positive reviews here*
>
> Just as the author found results from the methods in this book, so are the authors who have already purchased their copy, and putting the strategy to the test. If you are an Indie Author struggling to get the recognition you need to make it in this grueling industry, then you need this book.
>
> Don't wait! The discounted price ends in two days!

In this scenario, we have used psychology, and some simple, yet strategic copywriting skills to grab attention, and hopefully make those sales numbers rise. We had to focus on a few things here:

1.) We had to create the *NEED* for the book.
2.) We had to increase the confidence of potential buyers, and we did that by sharing the positives of the data sheets, and omitting the less flattering information.
3.) We had to establish the urgency to purchase at the discounted price; impulse buying for fear of a higher price later is a writer's best friend when marketing indie work, no matter the genre or format.

It can be a challenge to write positive copy when your stats aren't that great, but you are a writer, you can do it. If you want to learn more about writing copy, I suggest **"Copywriting Secrets" written by Jim Edwards.** I learned a lot about how to appeal to consumers, and while the book focuses on self-help books, and writing copy for that genre, his knowledge and experience is adaptable for fiction writers. The creative juices start flowing, and I personally learned how to adapt that information. What he has to say makes sense.

Please note, I have no affiliation with Jim Edwards, or his business. I have simply mentioned this because, I found the book helpful and educational.

Scenario two:

<u>Situation:</u> High reach, high engagement, low sales

<u>What this means:</u> Your ad doesn't five that "decision making" information. People are interested, even excited, and probably chewing their nails as they try to click the buy now button. However, they are still skeptical.

<u>Goal:</u> To remove the doubt of the consumer

Before I share my example with you, allow me to explain in advance how we remove the doubt of the consumer. We do this by establishing a rapport with them. Think about it, they've been scammed before, or they made a purchase that didn't follow through with their expectations. In my personal situation with this book, at first glance, it looks like one of many that they have watched the ads for on social media that didn't deliver what they expected, and were disappointed in their purchase.

I can recall being a freshman in high school, and having one of the best teachers ever. Before we began any assignment or test, she would always advise the class to perform their task with INTEGRITY. So, in this scenario, I am going to do just that. I am going to show an example of getting on the level of the consumer. Therefore, using this example to re-write a new ad/post/blog for a fiction work may be more of a challenge for you, but you are a writer. This is what you do.

Now, without further ado…

Let me set the scene for you:

You're scrolling through Facebook or Instagram, when all of a sudden, you see this ad for a book that promises you it contains all the secrets to become the next Stephen King or Laurell K. Hamilton. Not only will it happen, but it won't be stressful! You'll become an Amazon Best-Seller, and all of your dreams of becoming a profitable, fulltime writer will come true.

The best part? All you have to pay for this miracle book of secrets is shipping and handling cost! You anxiously await this book, and when it finally arrives, it's nothing more than a 175 page sales pitch for services that no starving artist can possibly afford.

What a let-down! Or, was it? Did you read those books with an open mind, or better yet, a realistic expectation?

I mean, the ad was a little dishonest, lying by omission in a sense because they didn't tell you that the secrets you paid for involved the websites and services that would cost you thousands of dollars to utilize. They may seem dishonest, but they weren't blowing smoke up your ass. The problem is, financially, you aren't there yet, and maybe even a little stuck on how to get there.

That my friends is where I come in. I bought the books. I read the books. I studied them. After all, I had plenty of time for reading and planning a marketing strategy thanks to COVID. When I started writing my marketing plan, I soon realized that I could sell this knowledge.

In short, I did the work for you. Therefore, I am proud to introduce to you "The Indie Author's no Bullsh*t Guide to Marketing on a Budget." Get the real information, the honest truth about what it costs to market effectively, when you're just starting out, or working to build you budget.

Now, I am not promising you a best seller's status on Amazon, but I am promising you the honest truth of what it truly takes, just to debut your book, as well as yourself to the world of readers.

Right now, I am offering my book to you for the cheapest price that Amazon will allow, (insert price here). This promotion is valid for two more days. The best part, it's not a 175 page sales pitch of services I can offer you. I will even share the secret before you buy. The cost of successful Indie Marketing is something more valuable than money, and that is time. Want to find out how best to use that time?

Click the link below, and grab your copy now, before the price jumps up because let's face it, just like you, I don't write for free. By the way, this book is also available in digital format, including free on Kindle Unlimited. So no matter your budget, you can read this book. One more thing; don't forget to write a review when you are finished.

Now, be honest, if you saw this ad on Facebook ™ or Instagram ™, you would be more inclined to purchase than if I said "I can guarantee you so and so!" It's completely honest. I related to the consumers, and I even told them they would have to spend a lot of time marketing to get to the point where more expensive and yes, effective services could be utilized.

Now, let's take a look at scenario three:

Scenario: Reach is high, engagements are high, and sales are high.

What it means: You've got the interest, you're getting the sales, so just get more!

Goal: Trigger the impulse buy- let your ad make the decision for the undecided; satisfy their need to see others were pleased.

The consumer group that fits this scenario, are the ones that wanted to wait it out, see if it sold, see if reviews got posted, follow the amazon rating, and decide if the purchase is worth it. Well, your book is preforming well, so this is what I like to call the bragging post. Brag about exceeding a goal and make sure you let the undecided consumer, the vigilant consumer know, "Hey, they did it. Don't you wanna keep up with the literary Jones'?" Since we don't have to work too hard for this one, the example will be short and sweet; you're only sharing the info they were waiting on.

> Indie authors everywhere are raving about that one book that gave them the secrets to effectively marketing their independently published work. I'm talking about *"The Indie Author's No Bullsh*t Guide to Marketing on a budget."*
>
> With no false promises of wealth overnight, this book, written by Ava Abernathy, AKA fiction author Dianah Brock, tells you just like it is. Marketing is a hard, grueling task that requires time and money, and dedication. She gives you the facts about the struggle you already know about, and how to turn those struggles into the beginning of success.
>
> Check out what reviewers already have to say:
>
> > (Insert two or three positive reviews here)
>
> For only two more days, *"The Indie Author's No Bullsh*t Guide to Marketing on a Budget"* is available for literally the lowest price Amazon will allow for a print edition. Don't be disappointed by another book meant to be for authors on a totally different financial level than you. You've sat back and watched the updates, so what are you waiting for? Click the link and grab your copy today. As always, don't forget to leave a review!

What we have done with this last and final ad/post/press release is we have eliminated that hesitation for the consumer. We have let them know that others have said, through reviews, messages, engagements, and other forms of communications that the claims of the book are legit. They know it's not just another scam, promising results that they will never see because the money isn't there to utilize the tools mentioned in many other books.

Now, I know that this can get confusing, and you may be asking, "This all sounds great, but how does any of these examples apply to fiction writing?" The answer is quite simple. If you use that famous Who, What, Where, Why, When, How method you learned in school for essay writing, you can also use it for copywriting some interesting ads.

If you are a writer, then you are a reader, and that means that you understand there is a need to be met with fiction books. Meet that need. I can promise you that the reason you wrote this book is the same reason your consumers will buy it.

Now, your last job to do for day four and five, is to engage with your audience. Be present on your social media platforms. Respond to questions. Thank your following for the comments and compliments they are leaving. Be active. This is honestly something I wish more celebrity writers did. It would mean a lot to me personally to have one of my favorite authors to reply to a comment with a simple, "Thank you for your support. I'm glad you enjoyed the book."

Paperback Launch
Day Five

This is the last day of your launch, and probably the easiest day as well. OK, that's not completely true; it's the day as far as tasks are concerned. Your nerves and length of your fingernails however, are a totally different story. This is the nerve wrecking day because at the end of it, you will see your results of your launch, or at least as close to your final results as you can get. The fact is, sales will continue over the next couple of days, and people are still seeing your ads and such.

If you want to go through and check your stats, feel free, but if you don't see the results of your efforts that you want to see, I don't want you to throw in the towel. Indie book marketing isn't for quitters. Indie marketing is for the optimist with a realistic point of view.

The truth is, every launch, every ad, every marketing attempt you try is hit or miss. Therefore, indie marketing is not for the dreamer within you that created the masterful story that you are now trying to sell to the world. Leave that side of you for the writer within. Therefore, if you decide to check those stats, do so from your business mind. Read those results as the business owner that you are.

Whether you have touched your stats or not, today, your main goal is to be both present, and engaging on social media. Make a simple post about the last day of your promotion in all of your groups where self-promotion is allowed. However, don't just post and run. Hang around the comment threads. Give the group a scroll through and remember when doing so, there are other indie authors out there trying to achieve the same goal as you. Show an interest in them, and they will show an interest in you. So cheer them on, be encouraging, and wish them well, just as you hope others will do for you. The golden rule definitely applies to indie marketing; **_Do unto others, as you would have them do unto you._**

Also, as you are visiting your groups and sharing your work, react to memes, find those moments where you can comment enough to strike up a conversation. You will always get sales or at least website or book views in some of the most unlikely ways.

I can recall a day, not long after I had launched my first audiobook, a political argument broke out in a writer's group where an independent blogger had shared their latest political blog. I can't remember exactly how I worded it, but I commented something to the effect of "Oh come on guys! This is not the place for political debates. Here! Watch my book trailer!" The response I got from that was overwhelming. Not only did I get responses in the comment thread, my followers grew, page views grew, and I even got three legitimate sales where I was only trying to give away free promo codes for my first audiobook.

Keep in mind, you can't ask for what you yourself are not willing to give to others. It's like this; if you are spending $0.99 on a kindle edition book every now and then, you can't expect anyone else to do the same for you. To expect something you are not willing to give is both immoral and unethical. The moral of these last few paragraphs is this; take today, day five to be social in the social media world.

At the end of day five, take a look at your stats. How do they look? Did your effort yield any results? What were those results? Now that the day is over, it's a great time to reflect, analyze, and absorb. I find my best results through a pros and cons comparison, but I do my cons first. Some of the cons you may see are:

- I didn't get the sells I wanted.
- My following didn't grow as much as I wanted it to.
- I didn't reach as many people as I wanted.

The reason I do this section first is that negativity is a very potent poison, especially for anyone creative, and if given the opportunity to administer the antidote, AKA positivity, you won't bring yourself down if you don't see the results you wanted to see. Some of the pros you could write in response to the cons are:

- I sold copies of my book
- My following grew
- My book reached so many more people than it would have without investing something monetary into my work.
- I interacted with new people who share my passion for writing.
- I just marketed a book and it actually sold.

- I wrote a book, published it, and sold it without an agent, advances, or contracts.
- My words are in the world forever. I have made history.

The best advice that I could ever give you would be to look at your indie author business with a positive mindset. Focus on all the positive outcomes that came to fruition through your hard work and efforts. Always focus on the freedom that indie publishing gives you. I believe Peter Parker's uncle Ben said it best; "With great power comes great responsibility." (Spiderman movie) However, in our world of creating, the saying should be worded a little differently. "With great talent, comes great sacrifice."

You have sacrificed a lot for this book, and if you followed the process, even without the desired outcome, you have still succeeded and moved forward in your journey as an author.

In closing this section, I want to say congratulations on a successful launch, because it was a success, no matter what the stats say, because you didn't quit.

Part Four Audiobook Launch

Audiobooks are quickly becoming a favorite method of "reading." In a world where everyone is extremely busy, sometimes our only time to indulge into our love of literature is when we are commuting to work, or doing the dishes. We don't have the time to crack open a good paperback while we relax for an hour or two before bed.

For indie authors, this is also another format for us to use to get our books out into the world. In my personal experience with audiobooks, I can honestly say that is where I found my success, and sales begin when I decided to take the plunge into that unknown realm of literature. If you chose Amazon for your print and digital books, then Amazon also has an outlet for audiobook production as well, known as ACX.

ACX.com is the place where writers and producers/narrators are brought together to find each other and join together in a partnership to create an engaging and captivating audiobook, no matter the genre. Writers set their project up on the ACX platform, and open the project for auditions for narrators to submit their reading from a portion of your book, or an audition script. Likewise, producers/narrators can record and upload samples so writers can browse through the vast selection of producers.

I could go on and on about ACX, and audiobook production, but that isn't what this book is about. This book is about launching the finished projects and gaining sales. However, if you have never tried audiobooks, visit Youtube ™ and search ACX University to learn more about audiobook production. Now, let's move on to launch prep.

Audiobook Launch Prep

Preparing for an audiobook launch is different than launching kindle or paperback edition books, and here is how it's different:

1.) You get zero say in the cost of your book, so there is no special price you can offer as a promotion.

While I love the ease and simplicity of initiating the partnerships between author and narrator, the lack of control I have over my book pricing doesn't settle well with me.

2.) You have to get creative with your press releases/ads to make it beneficial for the consumer.

Now, here are two ways you can do that, considering Amazon and Audible give you something to play around with. First, Audible offers a 30 day free subscription to try out their service. They provide the author and narrator with a bounty link they can share, which will give a new subscriber your book free. You will collect the royalty payment every time that happens, but the down side is, if the consumer doesn't pay the subscription fee the next month, and keep the service for the next 30 days, that extra 75.00 that is divided between the author and narrator is not paid.

    Your second perk that you have to work with is tied to your kindle edition of your book. Audible will offer your book at a discounted price if the consumer has already purchased the kindle edition through their whisper sync feature. Basically, the book is read to you as you read a long, or if you have to put your kindle down to brew a pot of coffee, the story doesn't have to stop. Therefore, I would check out my title on Audible and see what my whisper sync price is while planning my audiobook launch.

    Also, depending on how you covered funding for your project, you may receive twenty-five US promo codes and 25 UK promo codes to share with others, with the intent of receiving a review in exchange for the free copy. Before you ever get to the point of planning a launch for your audio book, you will want to get as many of these promo codes out as possible. You will also want to ensure that the recipient of those codes have posted reviews.

    With Audible and ACX lowering the number of promo codes author and narrator receive upon the release of their project, code distribution has become even more of a gamble. You have to be very careful who you give those codes to, and make sure the person requesting to review your book isn't what I like to call a code hoarder, a person who will request codes from literally every author or narrator that posts on forums, never post a review, and in some cases, will request a code for the same book a week later, meaning they don't even remember how many books they have claimed.

While twenty-five codes for each region isn't enough to gamble with, it's what we have. Therefore, I have a procedure to code distribution. When someone requests a code, I send a private message to them that reads, *"Thank you for requesting promo codes from Abernathy Books and Author Dianah Brock. Please redeem your code promptly, as codes are recycled every 72 hours. If you cannot provide a review within seven days, please do not claim the code. We sincerely hope you enjoy the audiobook, and look forward to reading your honest review on Audible."*

I also keep a record on a document to see who has reviewed and who has not. Please look to the next page to see the document.

Title	Recipient name	Request date	Code provided	Claimed	Review received

PROMO CODE RECIPIENT LOG

I allocate 20 of the 25 codes to be distributed for review purposes. I keep five to the side for my launch promotion. I will explain what we do with those a little later in the launch process. In the meantime, document every code you share. Fill in the chart, and follow up with the recipients after about seven days if you do not see the review. I will usually send a reminder note to their messages that reads, *"Hi! I sincerely hope that you are enjoying the audiobook you received. I can't wait to read your review! Hey, if you don't mind, could you send me a screenshot of your review? I would love to feature it on my Facebook Page and my blog. Thanks so much for your support."*

You have probably guessed at this point, that you will want to go on the hunt for reviews before you ever plan a launch. You need at least 5-10 reviews posted to audible before you "OFFICIALLY LAUNCH." Remember, we use those reviews in press releases, ads and videos. Once you have the reviews that you need, you are good to go on planning your official launch, and getting all the prep work done.

Audiobook Launch Checklist

The Day before

- ➢ Reviews are received
- ➢ Budget is set
- ➢ Press release/ad video made and approved via Facebook ™
- ➢ Dates are set
- ➢ Posts are scheduled in advance on your Facebook ™ page
- ➢ Posts are scheduled in your group
- ➢ Email is scheduled to be sent to subscribers
- ⬇ REMEMBER: Scheduling and pre-writing can free up a lot of your time to allow you to engage with your audience who are engaging with you.

Another useful tip is to be sure you have a positive partnership with the narrator/producer. Keep in mind that when they took that project on, that book became their baby too. Give them the credit where credit is due. I personally like to schedule an interview with my narrators during a promo week, so that readers get to hear details about both sides of production. Remember that they are more than just a voice. Include them. Beginning in the planning phase, include them. If you made advertisement photos, share it with them to promote themselves. Invite them to be a part of this launch, because without them, you wouldn't have anything to launch. If you and your narrator created the audiobook on a royalty share contract, they have just as much at stake in this race as you do, technically less to be honest. They produced the audio, but after that exclusive contract with ACX is over, you own the rights to the audio. Ok, I think I stressed that enough; be fair to your narrators.

Audiobook Launch

Day One

The first thing you want to check on Day one of your launch is that you paid ad is live. Once you've verified that you are "On the air." You will need to start posting in all of your groups. Copy and paste is your friend, especially after you copy the link to your ad and add it to your press release. Once you've added the link, go down the line of groups and copy and paste to your heart's content in each and every one where self-promotion is allowed.

Once you've done your group posts, don't forget to post to your personal page, and ask your friends and family to share the hell out of it. Ask them in the post, then go through messenger list and send it there too. Once Facebook ™ is covered, move on to Instagram ™.

In regard to Twitter ™ who limits your characters allowed in your tweet, go with something short and sweet.

For example: **Author Dianah Brock officially launches her Apocalyptic Thriller, in audio**

format. (Insert press release link for your blog post here.) Announcing your audiobook link on Twitter ™ in this manner will also drive more traffic to your blog site.

- Did you set up a Youtube Channel?
- Did you create or have a book trailer created?

If so, there is a second post for all of your social media channels later in the day. It's also a good idea to include the link to buy your audiobook in the description of your trailer on Youtube ™.

  A valid point to remember is that links that you use in your posts, press releases, video uploads, etc. can always lead to another place on the web where you can be found. The more visible you are on the web, the more of a "Big Deal" you appear. In a time where trending is trendy, that could mean positive results for your work, no matter the format. If readers and listeners begin to see you everywhere, then they are going to believe that they are missing out on something, and they will flock to it.

Finally, don't bother checking your ACX sales dashboard at the end of the day. You won't see any results updated for at least 24 to 48 hours. You may however, check on your promo code section to see if anyone has left any new reviews from the 20 promo codes you distributed weeks earlier.

Also, to save my fingertips, Lou's voice, and your time, I am going to go ahead and tell you that day two of your audiobook launch is going to go the exact same way as day one. There is no need to deviate from the plans of day one; not yet at least. With that being said, allow us to move on to Day three.

Audiobook Launch

Day Three

We will begin day three by checking our sales dashboard on ACX.com. Do you have any sales? If so, that's great! If not, remember not to panic. The only reason you are checking this first is to see where you stand, and to plan your next strategy. After you check your numbers there, pop on over to your promo code tab. The reason we are going here is to see if there are any new audiobook reviews. The last column of the chart will give you're your book's Audible star rating, and let you know if any new reviews have been posted for your title. If you have new reviews, go check them out, and see what listeners have to say.

New positive reviews can be a great tool for you to use on day three. Take a screenshot of the new reviews, and share them on your social media outlets. Now would also be a great time to feature those screenshots on a new blog post with a catchy title or headline, and post the link on Twitter ™.

Let's say for example that you received two new reviews. One is a five star, and one is a four star. We will still use both to write a positive blog post. Here is an example constructed from actual reviews that Lou and I received for Seal Evil: The Nine Gates. Check it out on the next page.

SEAL EVIL: THE NINE GATES AUDIOBOOK IS GAINING MOMENTUM!

In only three days since the official launch of Seal Evil: The Nine Gates, this comedic supernatural suspense thriller is gaining momentum, and more audiobook listeners are finding entertainment in the contents of the story.

In this fictional tale, we follow five strangers, who are joined together by supernatural abilities in order to stop a serial killer plaguing the streets of a small country town. However, this is no ordinary serial killer. They aren't killing for pleasure. They have a more devious and dangerous plan behind their murders.

Written by independent author, Dianah Brock, and narrated by Lou Petrella, this one is destined to quickly become a fiction fan favorite.

Just check out these reviews!

Five Star Review: "This story and audio was so spellbinding that I couldn't stop listening until the end. I would love for this book to be made into a movie."

Four Star Review: "Story was good. I am on the road for work and this book kept me interested throughout. Only found one predictable spot in the story line. Performance was great with characters distinct and clear. Would definitely recommend to friends."

Available on Audible, iTunes, and Amazon

For the past two days of your launch, your content has been the same. The last thing you want to do is leave your audience rolling their eyes at the repetition comes rolling across the screen. This will allow you to add to your blog, have fresh material to share, and even grab the attention of someone who wasn't really looking at your work yet. Share the headline with the link to your blog, and a copy of your book cover art on all of your social media sites. Remember to stay present, engaged, and available.

Audiobook Launch

Day Four

On days one and two, your content was the same. On day three, you released a blog post with reviews to grab some attention. On day four, I want you to step outside your comfort zone a bit. On day four, I want you to go to your events section, and schedule an online event for later that evening. What is the event? It's a live reading from your book, but only an excerpt.

I am a fan of prologues, even though a lot of authors these days frown upon them, I have been told by numerous readers that I could publish a book of nothing but prologues and they would be satisfied. I would never do that simply because I could never leave a story untold. Therefore, I would choose to read my prologue, and chapter one. However, if you are one of those authors that doesn't dabble in prologues, the first two chapters would be sufficient.

If you are not comfortable doing a live reading, as I do not because I read faster mentally, and my mouth can't possibly keep up with my brain, the idea of me reading aloud just doesn't sit well with me. Therefore, this is where I would have done one of two things:

- ➢ Collaborated with my narrator to join me on this live event and read it themselves
- ➢ Created a video, and used audio recordings of the sections.

Had I elected to create a video and attach the audio to that, I would have collaborated with my narrator in advance in the planning stage, and asked him or her to join me in the live event, and at the end of the video, participated in a Q&A between author and narrator, followed by answering any questions that viewers had in regard to the story or the production as well. If you check out my Youtube channel (simply search Abernathy Books) you will find interviews with three of the six narrators I have worked with.

Now, in reference to creating the video, you're probably sitting back screaming at your book, "I don't know how to do that!" Hold your horses there, I will include instructions for creating your own video in the back of this book.

What you probably didn't know, is that there is a website where you can get copyright free or public domain video clips that you can download for free and use your video editing software that actually comes standard on a windows PC to create this video. You can download the audio you plan to use from ACX.com as well, and attach the audio to the video.

Now, moving forward. Once you have your video premiere or live scheduled, go through your groups and share the link to the event page in all of the groups that allow self-promotion. Also share it on your Facebook Page ™ as well as your personal account. Go through your list and invite people to join the event. You can even send invites through messenger. Remember, copy and paste is your friend. Don't forget your other social media outlets as well.

TIP If you have a print copy, those remaining five promo codes, or even can spare $25.00 for a digital Amazon gift card, announce that there will be a drawing at the end of the event, and use these items as prizes.

Finally, follow through as planned. If you offer prizes, contact your winners from your drawing via private message and arrange for delivery. It is also helpful if you have a friend or family member who can watch the live and keep up with the names of the participants, writing their names down and putting those names into a container so a drawing can be done live. Close out your event by thanking everyone who participated, tell them how valuable their participation has been, and of course ask for their support in purchasing the book and leaving a review. Be sure to save the video when you're done. We will use it for day five.

Audiobook Launch

Day Five

The last day of your launch is finally here. Don't bother going to check on sales, reviews, or anything of that nature. Instead, spend the beginning of your day writing one more blog post discussing the live event that took place the night before. Share what happened, how you felt, how your narrator performed, and who all won prizes in the drawing. Finally, copy the link from the video of the event in the blog post so those who missed it can go back and watch.

Once your blog post is written and ready to go, post it everywhere, just as you have done with literally every post you have made during the course of these three launches. Don't forget when it comes to Twitter ™ Share the headline, then the link to the blog.

Stay available and present during the day. Engage with your audience, and for God's sake, keep your eyes away from ACX.com sales dashboard. At the end of the day, around seven pm. That is when you want to go down the list checking things out, not only on your dashboards for ACX, but also on KDP, and your stats once your Facebook ™ ad has ended. You may be surprised to find that you gained even more reviews, followers, kindle edition sales, paperback sales, or subscribers to your blog. Remember that every new change to the numbers is a positive outcome for you launch, and that there is no such thing as failure in the process because you tried, and you didn't quit. Once it's all over, reflect on the three launches. Write down everything you did, your thoughts on it, what you think you could have done differently, what did and didn't work for you, etc.

This book will come with a free PDF workbook, available on my website. In order to receive that free workbook, you must use the promo code WORKBOOK to be able to receive it. There will be a section in this workbook for each launch. Print it out and fill it out. Also, the pages will be standard size for documents, so it won't take much to print.

Conclusion

I hope that you have found this book to be the useful tool that it was intended to be when I began writing it. Remember that I cannot promise you a best seller status for your book, but we did make it a goal whether it happened or not. I hope that you have learned new marketing techniques, the way people think, and how to adapt the processes within this book to achieve your own success.

I hope that by sharing my experiences with you, you can push your book, and your writing business as a whole to new heights, and achieve goals that you didn't see yourself achieving prior to diving into the rambling honesty of this market. I firmly believe that if you followed this process, as closely as time and budget would allow, that you can walk away from launches with a smile on your face, and a winning attitude.

Keep in mind that the world of Indie Marketing is ever changing. It is important to read and research the industry as much as possible in order to keep up, so make time for that. Take that time to write, even if it's just a short 30 minutes after the family has gone to bed, or on your lunch break from your regular nine to five. Always make time to finish the story, and always make time to plan how you will share it with the world. Congratulations on your launch. I wish you well, and the next one will be even better. Remember, Indie Authors never quit.

Quick Reference Guide

- **For public domain photos and videos** visit www.pixabay.com. You must create an account to download the free content. However, please tip the artists that contributed.
- **For free cover art designing**, visit www.pizap.com you are allowed a free account, but the $7.99 subscription is worth it for the extra fonts and perks that are unlocked for members.
- **For free audio sound effects**, visit https://freepd.com/
- **To create your own book trailer,** type video editor in the search bar of your windows PC. Then open the app. After the app opens, add all of your video clips to the story board. It's pretty simple.
- **For professional sales ad photos:** subscribe to www.bookbrush.com you get a certain number of free images, but after that, you must pay for a subscription, which will become worth it as you grow.

Recommended Reading List

- ***Publish. Promote. Profit*** from Best Seller Publishing.
- ***Mastering the World of Selling*** by Eric Taylor and David Riklan
- ***Copywriting Secrets*** by Jim Edwards
- ***One Million Followers*** by Brendan Kane
- ***Thriving Scribes Planner*** by Brit Poe (Also recommend purchasing her Author platform Incubator program)
- ***Self Confidence- Daily habits for self-confidence, self-esteem, and self-development*** Available on Audible by: Perfect Self, narrated by Lou Petrella

www.ingramcontent.com/pod-product-compliance
Lightning Source LLC
Chambersburg PA
CBHW071403210526
45465CB00001B/235